Who Was
Coretta Scott King?

by Gail Herman

illustrated by Gregory Copeland

Penguin Workshop
An Imprint of Penguin Random House

As always, for Jeff—GH

For my sisters Marci, Karin, Shelagh, Teresa, and
Michelle, with love—GC

PENGUIN WORKSHOP
Penguin Young Readers Group
An Imprint of Penguin Random House LLC

Text copyright © 2017 by Gail Herman. Illustrations copyright © 2017
by Penguin Random House LLC. All rights reserved. Published by Penguin Workshop,
an imprint of Penguin Random House LLC, 345 Hudson Street, New York, New York 10014.
PENGUIN and PENGUIN WORKSHOP are trademarks of Penguin Books Ltd.
WHO HQ & Design is a registered trademark of Penguin Random House LLC.
Printed in the USA.

Library of Congress Cataloging-in-Publication Data is available.

ISBN 9780451532619 (paperback)   10 9 8 7 6 5 4 3 2 1
ISBN 9780451532633 (library binding)   10 9 8 7 6 5 4 3 2 1

Contents

Who Was Coretta Scott King? 1

The Scott Family 5

Starting School 18

Going Up North 31

Coming into Her Own 35

Meeting Martin 41

Back in Alabama 45

Change Comes Slowly 48

The Movement Builds 62

Birmingham and the March on Washington . . . 69

Marching in Selma 83

A New Direction 92

Life After Martin 97

Timelines 106

Bibliography 108

Who Was Coretta Scott King?

It was a cool and drizzly day in early spring 1968. Coretta Scott King stepped off an airplane in Memphis, Tennessee. Days earlier, on April 4, her husband, Martin Luther King Jr., had been shot and killed downtown in the city. Coretta was now a widow at age forty-one. She was heartbroken and tired, but determined.

Martin was the leader of the civil rights movement to give black Americans the same rights as white people. He had planned to lead a protest march in Memphis. Now he was gone. But the march was still being held.

Why?

Martin would have wanted it. Coretta knew that. And she knew she had to be there, too. She'd always been by his side when he needed her.

And he needed her now to carry on.

Some friends urged Coretta not to go. They feared her life would be in danger. She didn't listen.

At the march, Coretta and three of her children linked arms at the front of the crowd. And they began to walk.

The protesters—as many as forty-two thousand by one estimate—marched for about one mile. People lined the street as they passed. No one cheered or waved or shouted. They were too sad.

At city hall, there were many speeches about Martin. Then came Coretta's turn. She talked about his life as a husband and father. Finally, she said, "How many men must die before we can really have a free and true and peaceful society? How long will it take?"

After, her oldest daughter said, "Mommy, you were real good."

Coretta hoped her presence had given people strength. Being there gave Coretta strength, too. She felt more determined than ever to carry on the cause of civil rights. She'd always been Martin's partner in the struggle for equality. Martin believed that he and Coretta "walked down this path together."

That was true. Coretta Scott King had believed in peace and justice—right from the very beginning.

CHAPTER 1
The Scott Family

Coretta Scott was born on April 27, 1927, outside of Marion, Alabama, in the small town of Heiberger, Alabama. Sometimes the area is called the Black Belt because of its rich black soil. But in the 1800s, the term had another meaning. It referred to the black slaves who had once worked the cotton fields on large farms called plantations.

Their lives were harsh, filled with backbreaking work and cruel treatment.

Slaves were considered property. Like a horse or a piece of furniture. They had no rights. White owners could whip them, sell them, or work them to death.

After the Civil War ended in 1865, all slaves

Willis Scott

were freed. Like many others, Willis Scott stayed right where he was. In Alabama. In time, Willis managed to buy his own land. Over the years, generations of Scotts farmed those fields, working hard and raising families.

In 1920, Coretta's father, Obadiah "Obie" Scott married Bernice McMurry.

They built a small, plain home with two rooms: a kitchen and a bedroom. Soon, they had a family: Edythe, Coretta, and Obie Jr. Slavery had ended over sixty years ago. But life was still difficult for African Americans.

From Slaves to Sharecroppers

After slavery was abolished, plantation owners still needed workers. So black families rented small plots of land from former masters to farm. Instead of rent money, they gave landowners some of their crops. But the owners charged families for seeds and food and other goods. Often, sharecroppers owed more than they made. They never had enough money to buy their own land. Cruelly, they were still bound to masters.

In Alabama, and other parts of the South, black people were segregated from white people. That means laws kept them separated.

Obie worked at a sawmill, where logs were cut into boards for building. By the time Coretta was born, he had saved enough to buy a truck. Now he could work for himself, hauling trees.

Jim Crow Laws

From the late 1870s to the mid-1960s, African Americans in the South lived under racist laws called Jim Crow. Black people and white people had separate schools and parks, restrooms and water fountains, hospitals and businesses. It was called "separate but equal." But it wasn't. Black Americans suffered.

Then, in 1929, when Coretta was a toddler, the Great Depression hit. It was a time of great hardship throughout the United States. Millions of people lost jobs. And Obie lost work.

The Scott home only had a fireplace for heat and no running water or electricity. But the Scotts got by. They ate vegetables from their own garden, and had eggs from their own chickens. Everyone in the family worked hard. Coretta didn't mind.

She liked being busy. As soon as she could walk, she'd follow Grandfather Scott to the fields to help.

At around age six, Coretta started tending the family garden. By ten, she was working in the cotton fields. She felt proud of her cotton-picking skills. Strong and strong-willed, Coretta boasted she could pick cotton faster than any boy her age.

Coretta had fun, too. She was a tomboy. She loved being outdoors. Nothing scared her—not hitting wasp nests or baiting fishhooks with worms.

Indoors, music filled the Scott home. Coretta's parents had one of the first Victrolas, an early record player. They owned books, too. Her parents read nursery rhymes and fairy tales to Coretta, Edythe, and Obie again and again.

Faith was important to the Scotts, and much of Coretta's life centered around church. Every Sunday, men put on suits and women wore their best hats and dresses. The Scott children had to walk four miles to go to Sunday school.

Grandfather Scott would open the service by singing a hymn. Coretta loved the music.

It all gave Coretta a sense of pride and history. But there was a whole world outside Heiberger. It was filled with different rules for black people and white people. In elementary school, Coretta saw that for the first time.

Gospel and Spirituals

After the Civil War, many Southern black people formed their own churches. They featured a new kind of music: gospel. Gospel is rooted in songs called spirituals, created by slaves. The slaves sang about pain and faith in songs like "He's Got the Whole World in His Hands." Later, the gospel hymn "We Shall Overcome" became the song of the civil rights movement.

CHAPTER 2
Starting School

Coretta started at the Crossroads School in 1932, when she was five. The school was one big room with only two teachers for more than one hundred students. Students had to buy their own

books. There were a few blackboards, but not much else. It was nothing like the nearest white school.

She and Edythe walked three miles each way, no matter the weather. School buses were for white children only. When Coretta asked why white kids

got to ride on a bus, her mother answered, "It's just the way things are." But she didn't leave it at that. "You are just as good as anyone else . . . You get an education and try to be somebody. Then you won't have to be kicked around by anybody."

Coretta understood what her mother was saying. And she believed in standing up for herself, and for others.

Walking home from school that very first day, three classmates began to bother the sisters.

The boys were older and bigger. One pushed Edythe. "Don't do that!" Coretta cried, grabbing him. "She's my sister! Leave her alone."

They did.

But Coretta couldn't fight Jim Crow laws. When she went into town for ice cream, she had to use the store's side door. Then she had to wait for every white person to order. She could only get certain flavors: the ones no one else wanted. All that, and she had to pay the same price.

When Coretta turned ten, the Scotts were able to move into a bigger house with brand-new furniture.

Coretta, however, didn't live there full-time for very long. In September 1939, at age twelve, she joined Edythe at Lincoln School as a seventh grader.

Lincoln was a private school, ten miles away in Marion. The tuition: four dollars and fifty cents a year. The price was high for the Scotts. But the nearest black public school was twenty miles away from their new home.

At Lincoln, Coretta had to live with a black family in town. Once again, school buses were only for white students, and she had no way to travel.

Living away from home was a first for Coretta. But now Coretta went to a school as good as any white one. Its purpose was to inspire graduates to serve the African American community.

At her new school, white and black teachers worked together. But outside school grounds, racism was everywhere.

Marion was much bigger than Heiberger. Often, it was scary for Coretta to just walk into town. White teenagers would block the sidewalk, trying to force her into the street.

When she cleaned house for a white woman, the woman expected Coretta to use the back door. She had to act a certain way, too. Meek and humble. Fortunately, Coretta didn't work for that woman very long.

Coretta was in Marion on Thanksgiving night in 1942 when she and Edythe got a phone call: The Scotts' home had burned down! By then,

Obie was doing so well, some white people were jealous.

Obie had been threatened for years. Men with guns had pulled him off the road. Each time, he'd looked them in the eye and stood up to them in his strong, quiet way. And each time, he'd survived. Yet now, out of nowhere, a fire had burned down their house. Who had done it?

The police—all white men—did nothing. The Scotts had to move in with Grandfather McMurry for a while.

Not long after, in spring 1943, Obie set up his own sawmill. A white man wanted to buy it. Obie said no. "Well, it won't ever do you no good," the man told him. Two weeks later, the mill burned down. This time, Obie didn't bother with the police. He just came up with a new idea: a grocery store. The Scotts were determined to keep paying for the school in Marion.

When Coretta was a junior, she was able to

move back home. Obie turned one of his trucks into a school bus. Bernice drove, taking Coretta to school at Lincoln and picking up children along the way.

By then, Coretta had learned to play the trumpet and piano, and to read music at school. A gifted student, she took voice lessons, too.

Lincoln students traveled far and wide, giving concerts. They played for white and black audiences. Coretta saw how music could bring people together. Maybe, she thought, music was a way to change the world.

Coretta graduated from high school in 1945, the top student in her class. Edythe was already at Antioch College in Ohio. She encouraged Coretta to go there, too. It had only a handful of black students. That didn't stop Coretta. Still, she wondered: What would this new world be like?

CHAPTER 3
Going Up North

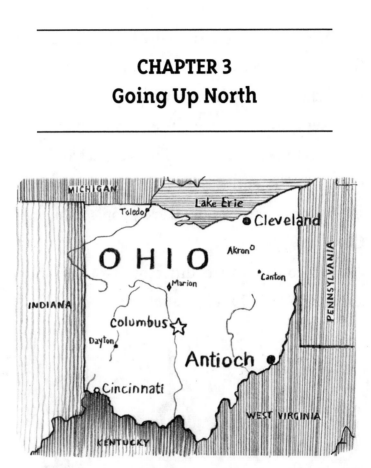

At Antioch, outspoken Coretta suddenly felt shy. It was all so different! She was used to a close, all-black community. Now she was among so many white strangers. Her roommates and her teachers were all white.

Most people were friendly. But Coretta's new friends didn't see that black people never had the same chances they had growing up.

They'd ask Coretta: "Why don't more black students go to college?" They expected her to speak for the entire race. And sometimes they'd make comments about black people that upset Coretta.

"Of course you're different, Corrie," they'd add, using her new nickname.

At first, classes were difficult. But little by little, she grew more confident. By senior year, Coretta was known around campus for her singing. She continued taking music classes and decided to study to become a teacher, as well.

As part of the program, she was supposed to teach in a nearby elementary school. However, parents of white students didn't want Coretta teaching their children.

Did anyone at Antioch stand up for her?

Sadly, no. No one would do anything. Not even the president of the college.

Coretta was stunned. Antioch was known for being open-minded and fair to all people. And still, there was racism.

Coretta ended up teaching at a school on the Antioch campus. It wasn't what she wanted. But what else could she do? She needed to finish the program.

"I have to face these problems. So I'm not going

to let this one get me down," she told herself. "I'll have to accept a compromise now. But I don't have to accept it as being right."

CHAPTER 4
Coming into Her Own

From being at Antioch, Coretta realized that if she wanted a better life, she needed more than education. She needed to have equal rights. She needed to push for change, for all African Americans. She joined the NAACP.

Coretta joined other organizations, as well. And in March 1950, she sang in a concert to

support black rights. The star of the show—famous actor, singer, and activist Paul Robeson—encouraged Coretta to keep performing.

When Coretta left Antioch the next year, she continued her studies at the New England Conservatory of Music in Boston. She had taken a room in a large house in Beacon Hill. It was in a lovely historic area of narrow, winding streets.

The National Association for the Advancement of Colored People

Formed in 1909, the NAACP was one of the first civil rights groups in the United States. Its mission: to make sure black people had equal rights.

The group brought cases to court to get unfair laws changed. Today, it has more than half a million members.

Beacon Hill

Coretta was worried about money. She had come to Boston with only fifteen dollars. She had won a scholarship. That helped pay for school. But she had to eat, too. Coretta took jobs doing cleaning and office work. Money came, too, from a surprising place—the state of Alabama.

Why would Alabama help out a young black woman?

There is a saying: Good can come out of evil. It means something wrong can lead to something right.

That's what happened to Coretta. Since Alabama didn't offer music programs to talented black students, the state was forced to cover some of Coretta's expenses in Boston. Finally, Coretta could stop worrying about money.

In Boston, Coretta was busy but lonely. And though there were no "whites only" signs in Boston, there were many places she didn't feel welcome.

Then a friend phoned. "Have you heard of M.L. King Jr.?" she asked. Everyone called Martin Luther King "M.L." at the time. The friend thought he and Coretta would make a good couple.

Coretta hadn't heard of Martin. But the friend explained he was studying religion at Boston University. At first, Coretta wasn't interested. She thought ministers were too serious. But finally, she agreed. She didn't know it then, but she was coming to the biggest turning point of her life.

Young Martin Luther King Jr.

Martin was born in Atlanta, Georgia, on January 15, 1929. His father was a minister, and the church was Martin's second home. An excellent student, Martin skipped two grades in high school, then graduated from Morehouse College, an all-black, all-male school. After college, he became a minister, like his dad.

CHAPTER 5
Meeting Martin

When Martin called, he talked nonstop. And at lunch the next day, Martin didn't impress Coretta in person, either. Not at first. But this time, when Martin started talking, she found him charming and sincere. They shared so many of the same thoughts and ideas. He wanted change and equality. He wanted to contribute to his race and to the world.

At the end of the date, he said, "The four things that I look for in a wife are character, intelligence, personality, and beauty. And you have them all." Right away, he knew he wanted to marry Coretta.

Coretta thought those were just words. He didn't even know her! But over the next few months, they spent more time together. Martin was fun to be with, open, and honest. Coretta was falling in love.

But did she want to get married yet? Back then, in the 1950s, most women had to choose between marriage and a career. Martin was going to be a minister. He wanted a stay-at-home wife who would be involved with his church and its events.

Coretta had career plans. She wanted to pursue music. What should she do?

Coretta knew this would be the most important decision of her life. In the end, she decided to marry Martin. And maybe, somehow, she could still have a career, too.

Coretta and Martin married on June 18, 1953, at the Scott family home. Martin's father, whom everyone called Daddy King, performed the ceremony. He was the minister of Ebenezer Baptist Church in Atlanta, the capital of Georgia.

Coretta had strong ideas about the words she would say at the ceremony. She wanted to leave out the part where the bride promises to obey the husband. So Daddy King did. Coretta also wore a blue dress, not a white wedding gown. She did things her own way.

Daddy King

After getting married, the couple returned to Boston to finish their studies. In 1954, Martin was offered a job at Dexter Avenue Baptist Church in Montgomery, Alabama.

After seven long years, Coretta was going back to the South.

CHAPTER 6
Back in Alabama

That September, the Kings arrived in Montgomery, Alabama's capital. Coretta bought a piano for their new home. She taught Sunday school. She began to feel at home. And soon, she was singing again in small towns.

Just a few months earlier, the Supreme Court had ruled that having separate schools for black children was unfair and had to stop. Many consider this the real start of the civil rights movement.

Martin knew that even with this ruling from the Supreme Court, change in the lives of black people would not come easily. He needed to work hard for that. The way he would do it was through peaceful protests. To begin, he focused on a church committee, a group dedicated to helping others. Right away, a class was started to show blacks how to register to vote.

Soon, Martin's reputation as an inspired speaker and leader grew.

One year after moving to Alabama, Coretta and Martin had a baby. They named her Yolanda, Yoki for short. It was such an important moment for the Kings—they were starting a family!

Another important event happened two weeks later in Montgomery. On December 1, 1955, a black woman named Rosa Parks left her job at a Montgomery department store. She boarded a bus and took a seat.

That one small act triggered huge changes for the South. And for the entire country.

CHAPTER 7
Change Comes Slowly

In Montgomery and across the South, the city buses had their own racist rules. The first four rows were for white riders. If those seats were full, white passengers could take "black" seats in the back of the bus. If African Americans were sitting in them, they had to give up their seat and stand. Anyone who refused was thrown off the bus or arrested.

That afternoon, Rosa Parks was sitting in a row reserved for black people. The bus became crowded and Rosa refused to give up her seat so a white man wouldn't have to stand.

She'd had a long day at work and was tired. It should be her right to keep a seat. Rosa Parks was arrested for what she'd done. After that,

groups like the NAACP were ready to act.

Martin met with black city leaders in Montgomery. They decided to boycott the public buses; that meant black people would stop riding them. Seventy percent of bus passengers in

Montgomery were black. If they all boycotted, the city would lose money. Many businesses would suffer, too. Black customers wouldn't be able to get to stores to buy anything. And if white businesses started to lose a lot of money, maybe then bus rules would change.

Because of Martin's work, the boycott was set to begin just days after Rosa Parks was released

from jail. Coretta was already up by five thirty that morning, anxious and excited. From a window, she could see a bus stop.

Finally, the first bus drove up and stopped. "Martin!" she called. "Come quickly!" No passengers were inside. The second bus was empty, too. Martin jumped into their car to check other bus lines.

At the end of the day, hardly any African Americans had ridden a bus. They walked to where they needed to go. They hitched rides. They took taxis. The boycott would continue until black people had the same "bus" rights as white people.

A new group was formed to lead the protest, and Martin was elected president. It was called the Montgomery Improvement Association.

Coretta and Martin understood that starting a boycott was risky. Some white people would do anything to stop black advancement. There could be violence. With Martin as a leader of the boycott, the whole King family might be in danger. Still, Coretta approved 100 percent.

The Kings' home turned into headquarters.

Meetings were held day and night. Coretta had newborn Yoki to feed and take care of, plus everyone else who came over. Coretta handled mail and phone calls, and made sure information was relayed.

She told Martin, "How happy I am to be living in Montgomery, with you, at this moment in history."

Weeks passed and the boycott continued. Black people still refused to ride the buses. City officials decided to get tough. They arrested Martin. They put him in jail.

What for?

He had been driving thirty miles per hour in a twenty-five-mile-per-hour zone. Coretta expected this. She'd even told him *not* to avoid being jailed. She knew his arrest would unite people and make big news all over the country.

Coretta was right. The boycott was covered in major newspapers. Martin was released that night.

Not long after that, Coretta was home, watching TV with a friend. Yoki was sleeping in the back room. Martin was at a meeting.

Suddenly, she heard a noise—a loud thud, then a blast rocked the house. Glass shattered. Smoke filled the air. Their home had been bombed!

As Coretta grabbed Yoki, the phone rang. Without thinking, Coretta answered it. "Yes, I did it," said a voice. "And I'm just sorry I didn't kill all you . . ."

Coretta hung up as neighbors streamed in to help. Martin hurried home as soon as he heard the news. He saw Coretta and Yoki were okay. Then he faced the crowd. "We must meet hate with love," he said.

Violence from black people wouldn't solve anything, he and Coretta knew. It would make everything worse.

The crowd quieted. The danger was over . . . for now. But what about the future? Coretta would face situations like this again and again. Did she have the strength?

Yes, she decided. Equal rights were too important. And her faith would keep her strong.

Her parents begged her to come and stay with them, away from danger. "I can't go," she said. "I want to stay here with Martin." She sounded braver than she felt.

The threats continued for months, and so did the boycott.

To mark the boycott's one-year anniversary, Coretta decided to raise money for the cause. She helped organize a concert in New York City. Coretta would sing.

How could she tell the story of the boycott for

the Northern audience? She remembered a time she'd performed in high school. Besides singing, she had read parts of books that talked about freedom. She could do something like that again! So she sang spirituals. She told real-life stories. One was of a tired grandmother who, rather than ride a bus, insisted on walking. Then she sang a song based on her words. "My feet are tired, but my soul is rested."

The concert was a huge success; Coretta had found a way to combine her passions: singing and justice. A few weeks later, Montgomery officials agreed to riders' demands. No more "whites only" seats on buses. Black people could sit wherever they chose. The boycott was over.

CHAPTER 8
The Movement Builds

The Montgomery Bus Boycott was a milestone for equal rights. Martin Luther King Jr. was now a national hero. He was away from home more and more. He had speaking engagements in other cities at rallies and protests.

Martin was helping to start a new civil rights organization, too. It grew into the Southern Christian Leadership Conference—the SCLC—and it was taking on other civil  rights issues besides transportation. Its basic belief: Nonviolence was the most powerful way to make change happen.

In September 1958, Coretta was home with Yoki and her second child, one-year-old Marty. Martin was in New York City, signing copies of a book he'd written. Coretta was getting ready to pick up her husband at the airport when a telephone call came. Martin had been stabbed.

Immediately, Coretta flew to New York. In the hospital, Coretta and Martin talked for hours. They agreed that the woman who had attacked him—a mentally ill black woman—needed help. Not punishment. And they came away more prepared than ever to take on challenges.

In late 1959, the family moved to Atlanta so Martin could work with his dad at Ebenezer Baptist Church. Soon after, a cross was set on fire on the Kings' lawn.

It was an act of hate to scare the King family. By now, though, Coretta felt ready for anything. She understood that standing up for a good cause came with a price.

Like many in the 1960s, Coretta was against America's involvement in the war in Vietnam. She joined in protests against the war. Not just as Martin Luther King Jr.'s wife. But for herself. Coretta Scott King. She even traveled to Switzerland to meet with leaders of other countries.

Still, raising her children was Coretta's main concern. When Yoki was five and little Martin three, they heard on the radio that Martin had been arrested at a protest.

The children asked, "Why did Daddy go to jail?"

Coretta answered, "Your daddy is a brave and kind man. He went to jail to help people."

She wanted her children to be proud. She believed in the cause. So much so, she wished she could be arrested, too. But of course that wouldn't have been wise. She had a growing family to take care of.

The Sixties

The 1960s were a decade of change, fueled by young people—both black and white—who wanted their voices heard. One issue they protested was the US involvement in the war in Vietnam—a small country in Southeast Asia. There were marches and sit-ins—sitting in public places and refusing to leave.

In January 1961, she and Martin had another son. They called him Dexter, in honor of their old church. And in March 1963, they had their fourth child, a girl named Bernice.

Even with four children, Coretta became more involved in causes than ever. It was for the future of her children, and everyone else's.

Once, the King children saw a TV ad for an amusement park. They begged to go. Coretta made excuses. Finally, she told them the truth:

The park "did not want colored people to come there . . . You see, we are colored."

Yoki began to cry. So Coretta told the children what her own mother had told her: that they were just as good as anyone else. Then she added, "This is really what your daddy is doing . . . he is trying to make it possible for you to go to Funtown, and for you to go any other place you want to go."

Where would Martin take his protest next?

CHAPTER 9
Birmingham and the
March on Washington

In early 1963, just after Bernice was born, Martin and the SCLC focused on starting protests in Birmingham, Alabama. The city of Birmingham was the center of business in Alabama. It was also known for its deep racism.

Martin helped plan demonstrations: a series of sit-ins, where African Americans sat at whites-only lunch counters. Protest marches to city hall. And boycotts of stores that practiced segregation.

On Friday, April 12, Martin was arrested. The weekend passed, and Coretta still hadn't heard from him. She knew black men could easily be taken from Birmingham jails—before they even had a trial—and killed.

So what did Coretta do?

She called and left a message for the president of the United States—John F. Kennedy.

Five o'clock Monday afternoon, the phone rang. Coretta answered. Little Dexter picked up  the extension at the same time, talking baby talk. Coretta realized who was on the other end. The president told her his office had looked into things. Martin was okay and would call as soon as he could.

John F. Kennedy

Fifteen minutes later, the phone rang again. It was Martin. He explained he'd been held alone in a small jail cell. But after the president got involved—thanks to Coretta—he was allowed to make a phone call, shower, and exercise.

Letter from Birmingham Jail

While in prison, Martin wrote a letter to white religious leaders who criticized him for being too impatient for change. He explained that after hundreds of years of injustice, it was impossible to wait patiently any longer. The letter has been published countless times and is a famous document for civil rights.

Immediately, Coretta went to Birmingham to make sure Martin was okay. Soon, he was released, but he chose to stay in Birmingham. Then on May 2, firefighters turned their hoses on civil rights marchers, knocking over men, women, and children, some as young as six. Police dogs attacked.

In times past, this type of violence could happen and people who weren't there would never hear about it.

But this was the 1960s, when TV cameras were on hand for news events.

The march was shown on the nightly news. Coretta watched along with the rest of the country. The horrifying scene turned the nation's attention on Birmingham. It forced the city to remove "whites only" and "blacks only" signs from public spaces and to come up with a plan to end segregation.

Martin came home to Coretta the very next day and they celebrated. The civil rights movement had just taken a giant leap forward.

In her autobiography, Coretta remembered voicing her thoughts at that time to Martin. Everyone wanted to hear him speak. So she said, ". . . you should call a massive march on Washington . . . I believe a hundred thousand people would come to the nation's capital at your invitation."

The idea had been floating around for some time. But now, Martin agreed, was the time to act on it. It would be a march for freedom, opportunity, and jobs. It would include people of all colors and all backgrounds. Martin would be the main speaker.

The march was set for August 23, 1963. It took many months of planning. The night before, Coretta stayed up late with Martin in their hotel room, working on his speech. When she woke in the morning, he was still typing.

The march began with a rally at the Washington Monument. It featured famous singers, actors, even baseball great Jackie Robinson. Then the marchers started the mile-long walk to the Lincoln Memorial.

Coretta gazed at the crowd, more people than she'd ever seen in one place. They'd been hoping for 100,000. But about 250,000 people had come. And just like Martin had wanted, they were black, white, and from all religions.

As soon as Martin finished, Coretta rose to her feet. She held his arm. This speech would make history. She knew that, and she needed to be close to him. She rode with Martin to the White House, where he and other leaders of the march were meeting with President Kennedy. Then she went back to the hotel. Waiting for him, she barely moved from the room. When he came back at 10:00 p.m., they talked for hours.

"I Have a Dream"

Martin's speech at the march is one of the best-known speeches in American history. It was a rallying cry for equality and unity, and inspired millions. Toward the end, he repeated the phrase "I have a dream," giving examples of people seeing past skin color. He ended with a vision: People of all backgrounds, holding hands, singing an old spiritual. "Free at last. Free at last. Thank God almighty, we are free at last."

How much change would actually come from the march? That question didn't have an answer. Not yet. So for now, she and Martin took time to celebrate the joy of a great moment.

CHAPTER 10
Marching in Selma

At the time, the March on Washington was the largest protest of its kind in US history. And on its heels came tragedy: On September 15, 1963, a bombing in a Birmingham black church killed four little girls. In late November, President Kennedy was shot and killed in Dallas, Texas.

Coretta felt shock and despair. The deaths affected her deeply. Yet she and Martin pressed on with their work. In so many ways, it was more important than ever. Great news came in July, when the new president, Lyndon B. Johnson, helped pass the Civil Rights Act of 1964. Across the country, in every state and city, segregation was now against the law.

Still, the work didn't end. By October, Martin

was so exhausted, Coretta brought him to a hospital to rest. The next morning, a reporter called the house. He told Coretta that Martin had just won the Nobel Peace Prize. She gasped.

The prize is one of the most celebrated awards around the globe, given to those who do the most to make the world a better place.

Coretta called Martin. "You are the winner!" she told him. At first Martin thought he dreamed the conversation!

In her autobiography, Coretta wrote that after the award ceremony in Oslo, Norway, she told friends it was "a blessing to be a coworker with a man whose life would have . . . an impact on the world."

Martin became busier than ever, and Coretta helped when she could, filling in for him at appearances. In November 1964, she gave her first Freedom Concert in New York City to raise money for the cause.

The concert told the story of the civil rights movement in readings and songs, ending with "We Shall Overcome." The theater was packed. There were people who had never gone to a civil rights rally, but they eagerly bought tickets to hear Coretta sing.

Over the years, she'd have many more concerts, raising thousands and thousands of dollars. But she was busy at home, too. In 1965, Atlanta's elementary schools had just been integrated. That meant Coretta could switch her children to a new school, one that before had been all-white.

Coretta knew her kids might feel uncomfortable, just as she had at Antioch College. But if the King children didn't attend an integrated school, wouldn't that go against everything the civil rights movement was fighting for?

That first morning, the King kids walked through the school cafeteria to register. A reporter stopped Coretta. The principal ordered him to leave, saying, "We don't talk to the press in this school."

Coretta later told a reporter where she would pick up the children after school. She thought something like this *should* be in the news. A peaceful integration of a school.

About the same time, Martin and the SCLC began a push to help African Americans vote. In order to vote, a person has to register their name on a list in their town. In many Southern states, black people trying to register had to wait in line for hours at a city office. Then, just before their turn came to register, the office would close.

So Martin planned another march. It would start in Selma, Alabama, and go to Montgomery, fifty-four miles away. It would take days. Coretta was pleased. Selma was near her hometown.

On March 7, protesters began to march. Martin was home in Atlanta. Everyone had agreed he should avoid arrest. That way, he could stay out of jail and direct the protest.

Martin wasn't expecting violence. But state

troopers attacked the marchers with clubs and
tear gas. They couldn't go on. Horrified, Martin
left for Selma right away, to plan another try.

Coretta was terribly worried. She'd heard rumors that Martin would be killed. And she was clear across the country, performing in a series of Freedom Concerts. She told a friend, "I have to resist worry. We know what we are doing is right."

On March 9, Martin started the second march. Once again, state troopers blocked their way. Fearing for people's lives, Martin called it off.

That night, a white minister from Boston was murdered by white segregationists. Why? He had eaten dinner at a black-owned restaurant.

The nation reeled. Something had to be done. President Johnson sent troops to Selma to protect the marchers.

Now thousands of people streamed into Selma to join the protest. Coretta, finished with her tour and speeches, arrived, too. By the march's last leg, the crowd was fifty thousand strong.

"Oh, it was good, very good," Coretta said later.

She marched past Dexter Avenue Baptist Church . . . past her parents who were cheering in the crowd, right up to the state capitol.

She saw Rosa Parks on the platform. She thought about the years since the Montgomery Bus Boycott. Yes, there had been terrible trouble along the way. But civil rights workers had made it this far. And they would make it further still.

CHAPTER 11
A New Direction

President Lyndon B. Johnson understood the power of the movement. After the Selma march, he saw to it that Congress passed the Voting Rights Act of 1965 on August 6. It outlawed all discrimination in voting practices.

Now Martin looked to the North. What could be done for the African American community in states there? There were ghettos in northern cities, run-down areas, where only poor African Americans lived. Most had nowhere else to go. White neighborhoods were keeping them out.

Racial tensions were running high. Even with the gains in civil rights, African Americans felt frustrated that there was still such a long way to go. Many were fed up. They wanted to strike back. They no longer believed that peaceful protests were the answer. Riots started. Fights broke out. Property was destroyed. Martin and Coretta understood why this was happening. But they still believed violence wasn't the answer.

In early 1966, Martin rented an apartment in Chicago, in the heart of a poor community, to try and calm people by being there. Coretta brought the children that summer. The apartment was small and dingy, and the neighborhood dirty. It was far different from the life the Kings knew in Atlanta.

Still, even living in those conditions, Coretta knew her family had it better than most. Some families didn't have heat or water.

Over the summer, she and the children went to rallies. They listened to Martin speak. But it was a difficult time, with rioting right on their street.

In late August, an agreement for fair housing was finally reached. It became easier for black people to get loans to buy homes. But little good came of it. No one would sell to them. Riots continued, and Martin grew discouraged. "I believe in you," Coretta told him. "If that means anything."

"Yes," he answered. "It means a great deal."

Martin kept searching for a solution. Although he was against violence, he saw that "A riot is the language of the unheard." He thought more jobs could be the answer. For integration to be successful, black men, women—and everyone!— needed better-paying jobs. So he took on more projects. He traveled. And whenever they could, Coretta and the children traveled with him.

In spring 1968, Martin went to Memphis, Tennessee, to help sanitation workers get better pay and working conditions. Coretta woke up early the morning he left. She followed him to the door and kissed him goodbye. It was an ordinary goodbye, she thought.

But she was wrong.

CHAPTER 12
Life After Martin

Later that day, April 3, Martin appeared at a rally in Memphis. He gave one of his most famous speeches, saying, "I've been to the mountaintop . . . And I've seen the Promised Land. I may not get there with you. But I want you to know tonight, that we, as a people, will get to the Promised Land."

The next night, Coretta got the phone call she'd been dreading: Martin had been shot, standing on his motel balcony. Eventually, James Earl Ray was arrested, a white man already wanted for other crimes.

Meanwhile, Coretta was already booking the next flight to Memphis.

At the airport in Atlanta, she heard her name

over the loudspeaker. She knew what it meant.
Martin had died. Part of her couldn't believe it.
But part of her could. She stood in the airport,
crying.

Then she went home to be with her children.

President Johnson called Coretta to say how sorry he was. On TV, he spoke to the nation about Martin and his death. Soon, thousands of people came to the King  home to pay their respects. Most hadn't known Martin. But they knew he gave his life to make the world better. The entire country was grieving.

Coretta spoke to reporters. She wanted the world to know that Martin hadn't been afraid of death. He was only thirty-nine. But the number of years hadn't mattered to Martin. What mattered was how well he lived them.

Coretta flew to Memphis to march in his place at a rally on April 8. But she didn't stop there. With Martin gone, she needed to do so much more.

Just weeks after he died, she spoke at an antiwar rally in New York City. The next month, she led a Mother's Day Parade through Washington, DC, to support poor families. The month after that, she spoke to thousands in front of the Lincoln Memorial, where Martin had given his "I Have a Dream" speech in 1963.

Then she had an idea: to build a memorial center for Martin, to keep his legacy alive, and to fight for civil rights. In 1968, she opened an office in her basement. She hired a staff. She collected his papers and books. She wanted this new center to display information on the entire movement.

To include classes and programs to teach nonviolent protest. To give out scholarships to deserving students.

It grew bit by bit, becoming the Martin Luther King Jr. Center for Nonviolent Social Change. In 1981, it moved to a national historic park in Atlanta, in the neighborhood where Martin had grown up. It included his childhood home, Ebenezer Baptist Church, and his grave site.

At the same time, Coretta worked tirelessly to create a national holiday on Martin's birthday. That happened in 1986.

And Coretta kept marching, kept speaking, kept fighting for people's rights. All over the world, she met with royalty and heads of government. She was a leader, known everywhere. In 1985, she was jailed for protesting South Africa's harsh segregation laws.

Coretta's last appearance was at a dinner honoring Martin's birthday, on January 14, 2006. She'd been battling cancer, and a stroke had left her unable to speak. But her strong presence was felt. Two weeks later, she died.

Four presidents attended her funeral. Around the world, people mourned. She had given so much and cared so much—about black people, white people, women, children, the poor. Everyone under the sun.

And her belief in peaceful protest, as well as her message of racial justice, will always be remembered.

At her funeral, one speaker took the words of a famous African American spiritual. "She was a woman born to struggle. And she has struggled, and she has overcome." Like the words from the song, Coretta Scott King had gone on to victories . . . and she had never been afraid.

Timeline of Coretta Scott King's Life

1927 —	Coretta Scott King is born April 27
1945 —	Goes to Antioch College in Ohio
1953 —	Marries Martin Luther King Jr.
1954 —	Moves to Montgomery, Alabama
1955 —	First child, Yolanda, is born
—	Helps start the Montgomery Bus Boycott
1957 —	Second child, Martin Luther King III, is born
1959 —	Moves to Atlanta, where Martin is a pastor at Ebenezer Baptist Church
1961 —	Third child, Dexter, is born
1962 —	Serves as delegate at an international peace conference in Switzerland
1963 —	Fourth child, Bernice, is born
—	Marches at the March on Washington
1964 —	Holds first Freedom Concert in New York City
1965 —	Joins the Selma March
1968 —	Leads Memphis march in Martin's place after he is killed
—	Establishes Martin Luther King Jr. Center for Nonviolent Social Change
1985 —	Is arrested in Washington, DC, for protesting segregation in South Africa
2006 —	Dies on January 30 at age seventy-eight

Timeline of the World

1927	Charles Lindbergh makes first nonstop solo flight across the Atlantic Ocean
	The Jazz Singer premieres, ushering in "talking" movies
1939	World War II begins
1947	Jackie Robinson becomes first black player on a Major League Baseball team
1954	Supreme Court rules school segregation unconstitutional in *Brown v. Board of Education*
1955	Ray Kroc opens the first McDonald's in Des Plaines, Illinois
1960	Seventeen African countries gain independence from European rule
1962	Astronaut John Glenn is the first American to orbit Earth
1963	President John F. Kennedy is assassinated on November 22
1965	President Lyndon Johnson signs the Voting Rights Act of 1965
	First US combat troops sent to Vietnam
1968	The computer mouse, invented by Douglas C. Engelbart, and the world's first jumbo jet, the 747, are both introduced
1985	Wreck of the *Titanic* is discovered
	Michael Jordan named NBA Rookie of the Year
2006	Construction begins on One World Trade Center in New York City

Bibliography

* Books for young readers

*Bader, Bonnie. *Who Was Martin Luther King, Jr.?* New York: Penguin
   Workshop, 2008.

Bagley, Edythe Scott, with Joe Hilley. *Desert Rose: The Life and Legacy of
   Coretta Scott King.* Tuscaloosa: University of Alabama Press, 2012.

King, Coretta Scott. *My Life with Martin Luther King, Jr.* New York:
   Henry Holt and Company, 1993.

*Krull, Kathleen. *What Was the March on Washington?* New York:
   Penguin Workshop, 2013.

*Medearis, Angela Shelf. *Dare to Dream: Coretta Scott King and the
   Civil Rights Movement.* New York: Puffin Books, 1994.

Vivian, Octavia B. *Coretta: The Story of Coretta Scott King.* Minneapolis:
   Fortress Press, 2006.